One Poem

One Poem

Christian McPherson

NON
CANADA

Publisher's note: This book is a work of fiction. Names, characters, places and incidents are either the product of the author's imagination or are used fictitiously, and any resemblance to actual persons living or dead is entirely coincidental.

Library and Archives Canada Cataloguing in Publication

McPherson, Christian, author
One poem / Christian McPherson.

ISBN 978-1-988098-38-8 (softcover)

I. Title.

PS8625.P53O54 2017 C811'.6 C2017-904643-8

Printed and bound in Canada on 100% recycled paper.

Now Or Never Publishing
#313, 1255 Seymour Street
Vancouver, British Columbia
Canada V6B 0H1

nonpublishing.com
Fighting Words.

We gratefully acknowledge the support of the Canada Council for the Arts and the British Columbia Arts Council for our publishing program.

For Marty, Molly, and Henry

Contents

One Poem

This is how it begins
with a kiss
and a song sung
the resonance of a medieval choir
and the din of skyscrapers

it begins with
the basketball falling through the netting
without touching the hoop
the cry of an orgasm
and the inhalation coming out of the water

it is beauty
it is everything
this poem

if I only could write one poem
this would be it

if I could only write one poem
this would be it

it would be a gift
it would be my heart
my tears
the world

it would be for me
but really it would be
for you

I would build it with yoga and math
sculpt it with ecstasy
and use a divining rod
to gather all the tears
shed by broken first loves

I would dump them into a blender
with rose pedals and cinnamon
pour it into a lowball
and drink it like Dorothy Parker
to invoke the sensibility of Ondaatje
and the delicate reverberation of Gluck

I would write it with such care
with such love
my hands would shake as I type

if I only had one poem to write
this would be it

I'm a liar.

One Poem

This is how it begins
in a laundromat
with a young man finding a poem
lying on the grey melamine
card table in the corner
where he normally studies
while his clothes
do the wet rollercoaster orgy

he picks it up
and reads the words
his teeth appear
like a movie screen
as the curtain of his lips
stretch and elevate into
the upper flesh of his face

he is smiling

he runs to the payphone
because he lost his cell
and dials his girl's number

her voice squeaks
and modulates
like a trailer hitch
bouncing on a dirt road

she has been woken up

he reads her the poem
and it makes her laugh
and then cry

he reads it again
slower this time
and she transcribes it
on her laptop

it goes Facebook viral

an anonymous billionaire
hires a detective
to find the poet
he finds the young man
with the poem
the detective brings it to the lab
for analysis

they find traces

Socratea exorrhiza
the Walking Palm
            the detective flies to South America
            where there are flying bugs the size of hats
            and beetles the size of shoes

he avoids a wardrobe malfunction
and gets men with machetes
to cut through to the other side
of Jim Morrison's lyrics
red tape
and the nasty jungle floor

there in a clearing
is a small dilapidated shack
a man appears in the doorway

looking like he has been
working under a car for the last
twenty years

he pulls the cigar from his mouth
and spits like he hates the earth

the detective passes the man the poem
and asks if he wrote it

the man replies, "What if I did?"

"You're famous then."

"Then I didn't," says the man
turning around
and he walks back into his shack
like a duck walking into a bar

the detective smiles his gumshoe smile
takes out his lighter and lights a corner
of the greatest poem
ever written.

One Poem

A whisper
secrets of love
passcodes and hidden keys
to a map
which leads to my heart
to my idea of the truth

if I could write only
one poem
what would it say?

it would speak wholly
of love
for my time with you
with our children

if I could write only
one poem
after
when I was done
I would give it to
a Japanese origami master
where he would
transform it
into the most beautiful
intricate paper swan
and then I would hop a train
to the ocean
and I would charter a boat
and I would take my bird
out to deep water
and let her go

I would watch her
bob up and down
doing the trampoline mamba
until her wings become water logged

I would watch her
until she disappeared
below the waves.

One Poem

Who would want to read
the artist's process
the evolution
if I put it on display?

am I merely a stripper
with a five dollar bill
hanging out my ass
or is this the real deal?

real deal—ha!

I have beer in my fridge
and food in my cupboards
and my only concern is
            am I going to win the Acorn-Plantos Award

the people don't give a good fuck about it

this poem
my jealousy
my insecurity
an armpit stain
embarrassingly smudging
this book.

One Poem

I'd use solar panels
to collect all the sun
which shines out of
all the optimists' assholes
every good morning

I'd use windmills
to collect all the hot air
from blowhards
and pretentious goons

I'd use Frankenstein cables
and attach them to the poet
who will write the greatest poem
of his life
the only poem

I'd pull on the giant lever
hang off of it like Buster Keaton
until it slowly slides down
until it clicks ON

the poet would do his Jiffy-Pop
twist and shout
the mental patient belts of beige
holding him in place

I'd free him
and he would immediately
find the computer
and begin to type

when he was done
he'd find the saddest
tallest building in the city
he could
and then he'd jump off
with the poem pinned to his shirt

I'd bury him with abandoned childhood toys
and all the wedding rings
tossed into all the rivers and lakes and oceans
from around the world

I'd read his blood-stained poem
and toss it too
into the grave

I would hear
the sounds of metal
slicing into the earth
the ring of the shovel
as I whacked the soil
packing it tight

the tombstone would read
"Art is dead."

One Poem

It begins with the sound of the rain
and the moan of the wind

it begins with my eyes closed

I can feel your radiator body
hear your gurgling pipes

blankets stir
from other rooms
the sound of small feet
soft against the floor
make their way to us

our children have
climbed into our bed
for a morning cuddle

this is everything important

and now it is written
and now it is done.

One Poem

This is how it begins
with one word
the first step on a journey

the words will grow
with the tenacity of vines
with the speed of a plague
with the splendour
and the expanse of the rainforest

you will be swept up in a tide
and it will carry you to foreign lands
          to mountain tops

the words will take you
from the earth
to the moon
to the Milky Way

you will become the cosmos
you will become everything
know everything

the poem will fall from your limp hand
your knees will buckle
and you will collapse

the ambulance will come
and take you away

somebody will pick up the poem
put it in the recycle bin
and it will become
yesterday's news.

One Poem

If I could write only one poem
it would be so avant-garde
so cutting edge
that it would make
the emperor's new clothes
look like a thick fur coat

it would make rap stars
pop bottles in bars
drink Bloody Marys
jump off ferries
commit harikari

it would make academics
open a new branch of study
make philosophy muddy
make chaos string theory look fuddy-duddy

it would make fashion models
hit the all-you-can-eat buffet
turn straight men gay
put time travel back in the heyday

it would make Finnegans Wake
look like an easy oven cake
make reality fake
cause vegetarians to eat steak

it would be so Manzoni
no phony baloney
give impotent men a boney
give bald bees an over comby

THIS IS NOT A POEM
understanding is paramount

giggle fart puke.

One Poem

It begins with holding my daughter's hand
as we walk through
the last days of autumn

leaves like soggy cereal
the wind an ice cube dropped
down your shirt

the clouds are Pangaea grey yogurt

it's so perfect
I have difficultly
understanding it

difficultly understanding
it will one day
be gone
that one day
I'll
be gone

nothing left except
this poem.

One Poem

I will gather the greatest scientific minds
of my generation
and have them create a machine
with new technology

it will take my poem
and turn it into a liquid
    into a gas
    into an electronic pulse
    into a wave

they will create a chamber
that will make Brundlefly drop his labium

you will enter it
be wrapped in translucent blankets
    with wires running through them like veins

they will take my poem and inject you
    gas you
    radiate you
    bombard you

the poem will melt to your skin
    enter your blood stream
    go down river
    and fuse with your DNA

when you walk
    it will always be with a metaphor

when you eat
    it will always taste like music in your mouth

when you listen
    you will hear the complexity of emotion
    and the infinite sound of silence

when you speak to strangers
    they will fall in love with you

when you stand on the corner
    waiting for the light to change
        you will cause accidents
        waiters will spill their trays
        workman will hammer their thumbs

when you cry
    your tears will stain your clothes like beet juice

when you laugh
    it would be the raw laughter of children

and when you die
    your body will dissolve into flowers
    and the people of the earth will know the words
    of the poem in their native language
    they will know love
    but only for an instant
    then the memory will fade
    the world will come into focus like developing film
    and they will forget the words
    and the feeling of love will be lost

    your petals will blow away in the wind.

One Poem

I would write it
photocopy it a million times
post it on every telephone post
            on every lamppost
            on every bulletin board

I would be arrested
there would be a backlash
T-shirts would be made
people would die in protests
academics would debate
science would be questioned
and all religions would denounce it

ten years later
I'd be sitting in a bar
and a man would walk up to me
and say "Aren't you that guy
            that guy who wrote
            that poem?"

"Yeah," I'll say, "that's me."

"Yeah," he'll say, "I liked that one.
            Thought it was pretty
            good. Nice to meet you."

"Yeah," I'll say shaking his hand, "You too."

and I'll go back to drinking my beer.

One Poem

If I could write only one poem
it would begin with the tenderest of kisses
with peppermint breath
and the smell of aftershave
which would remind you of your grandfather
the one who took you to the corner store
for a comic book and a bag of chips

the music would begin
a large string section
would melt your heart
as we climb into a carriage
drawn by white horses
and we would once-around
the park with James

I would tell you how much
I love you
how you mean
the world to me

I would write it all down
and present it to you
in this one
and only
poem.

One Poem

This is how it begins

with nothing

not a single good idea

my writing impotence

laid out

a dirty skid mark in my underwear

embarrassment

shame.

One Poem

The barker hollers
points with his stick
to the big tent
behind him

he yells at passersby
about the poet inside
about how he is about to read
the greatest poem ever written
the greatest poem in the world
the only poem you will ever need
to hear

hurry hurry
he barks
the show is about to begin

and it begins like this
with a hush falling like dead weight
over the audience

the poet walks across the stage
with the shadow of Presley
the accuracy of royalty
and with such poise and grace
it causes several members of the crowd
to tremble violently in their loins

he looks down at the pulpit
looks down at the paper before him
and begins to read

a woman stands and gasps
and then faints
after the first line

by the end of the first stanza
many women have collapsed
a fight among two priests
has broken out in the back

by the end of the third stanza
children are crying
dogs are barking
and a full-out brawl is in progress

a salad bar is being tossed
at the poet's head

he gracefully dodges a green pepper
sidesteps an eggplant
while a chorus of patrons scream
for their money back

before he can finish
he runs off the stage
being pelted in the back
by florets of cauliflower
and a violent rain of Brussels sprouts

outside it's raining
the ground muddy
and the poet slips
falls
and the pages in his hand

go all paper airplane
crash landing in the mud
as the circus elephants
lumber by

the poet
lying in the mud
watches in disbelief
watches in horror
watches as his stomach delivers
an extra large combo wave
of nausea and knots

the pages disappear
picked up and tossed about
like canned goods
of a robotic assembly line

after they have marched away
nothing but a few tattered pieces remain
strewn in the mud
marshmallow pieces of a chocolate cookie

the poet stands
knowing he can't recreate it
knowing he will never be able to do it
again

he walks to the local bar
orders a strong drink
and drinks his drink

a young woman
with eyes like a glossy brochure
sits at the end of the bar
watching the poet
she thinks he just might be
the saddest man in the world

she walks over to him
sits down beside him
and says "hello."

One Poem

The language would have to be exquisite
each word a piece
of ice-cold strawberry cheese cake
placed on your tongue

the imagery so Instagram
so baroque ceiling
so forty thousand feet awestruck
that when you read it
you could feel the salty breeze
raise the hairs on the back of your neck
the smell of the ocean enveloping you

it would have to tell a story
a proverb
it would have to make you laugh
until you spilled your guts
          a river of joy buzzers
                    whoopee cushions
                              and exploding cigars

it would have to make you wonder
how it was possible

it would have to speak volumes
          11 on the Marshall stack scale

it would have to be
          all the things I could never
          possibly give you
          all the things I could never write

it would have to be my best attempt
        a Hail Mary
        a perfect storm
        dumb luck

it would be homage
        cliché
        desperate

it would have to be
        the last thing I could write.

One Poem

It wouldn't be a poem
it would look like a poem
sound like a poem
but really
it would be
secret instructions
on how to build
miniature robotic insects

once built
they would fly into the homes
of the 1%

they would fly into churches
mosques
and temples

they would fly into the ears
of those Thurston Howells
of those robe-wearing zealots

these robot bugs
would bore into their brains
would lay larvae of love and compassion
would perform the dance of drones
to let them know
where all the poor people are
where their money could be
best spent
how science could give them
clean water and a pat on the back

it would be Invasion of the Scrooge Snatchers
and suddenly
every day would be about menu choices
and how do we get across the galaxy?

this would be my one and only poem.

One Poem

It would rip out your cerebral cortex
shellac it with the drool of mental patients
collected with buckets like tree sap
it would resurrect Timothy Leary
          Ken Kesey
          and Dennis Hopper from the dead

it would M.C. Esher your mind
give you a split personality
and a deep neurosis

it would be deemed too dangerous
too unsafe for human consumption

biker gangs would reprint it
sell it underground
kids would drop out of high school
people would move in whole new directions
communes would form
on outlying farms
there would be naked people
and songs sung
with acoustic guitars
sung with authenticity and conviction
that the world is fucked
and this was the last vestige
a return to nature

they would be largely ignored
deemed mentally ill

committees would be formed
legislation would crawl forward

swat teams and raids would ensue
deprogramming
and someone would hug her daughter
wrap her in a blanket at the side of an ambulance
while the barn in the background
burned

a poet would be arrested
in a foreign land
blindfold
cigarette

BANG!

One Poem

I'm the poet rock star
Bukowski in the bar
McQueen driving his car
here to deliver
an atomic payload
in your lap
a rap
a slam
Bam!
double tap with Bond's Luger
cut you like Freddy Krueger
split your mouth wide
slice you like Julia Child
duck
come back up
with an unexpected right
this isn't a fight
this is a nuclear war
jihad knocking at your door
I give you more
expose myself like Morrison
make you scream
like you saw a shark fin
get you shaking like Parkinson's
because this poem
will exterminate all others
your weak lyrics it will smother
stab them like Norman Bates' mother
you don't stand a chance with me
like picking a fight with Bruce Lee
Jet Li
a swarm of bees
leave you stung

leave you hung
like an Eastwood spaghetti western
take the best room
at the Best Western
get room service to bring me
spaghetti
and their best toasted western
hold the mayo
I'm going put you in the clinic
get a cane
for your brain
you will Google my name
like an internet stalker
you'll need a walker
rhymes so raw and bare
you'll need a wheelchair
give you grey hair
make you cry "No fair!"
put you between a cub
and his momma bear
rip your poems apart
throw them in
the discount bin
put your shit in the dollar store
make you holler "No more!"
make my fists sore
conducting John Williams's score
a requiem
for your funeral service
make everyone else nervous
get 'em to dial 911 with their phones
all the ladies will moan
all the men will groan

when they read this
one
and only
poem.

One Poem

What five books of poetry
        would you take to the island?
smiling
your top five CDs please?

how could there ever be
        only one poem?

a futile exercise
a gimmick
a fraud
the barker on the corner
charlatan

who feels dirty now?

this whole business
a squandering of time

don't you know there are bridges to be built
rivers to cross
items to be understood and be counted
ducks to put into rows?

don't you understand
such a silly thing
will get you nothing
but the old tar and feather
routine?

mocked by my peers
all my fears
laid out on the light table
an x-ray
a fashion shoot

my book of poems
          is this the best he could do?

One Poem

It began
with the sensation
of the first big drop
of the rollercoaster
a free falling elevator
drop zone
then there would be
          antigravity

          floating

ice-cream in root beer floats
dissolving carbonated memory
we did everything that day
rode all the rides
          jockeys of the fairgrounds
had our pictures taken
          with the stars
watched 2270000 litres of water
          fall per second

there were volcanoes
made of chocolate fudge brownies
spewing hot fudge

that day scarred my brain
          with jellybeans
mutated my DNA with giggles
and forged elation into muscle memory

it ended with a Ferris wheel
and fireworks
and a smile
you could hook an eighteen wheeler
tracker trailer to

the only smile I will ever need.

One Poem

This is how is begins
          with an introduction
          a seduction

the words will whisper
          so gently
          a breeze off the salty water

but the winds will
          pick up and exterminate
all your inhibitions
the words turning into a monsoon
socialized medicine of Bethune
all your body parts equal
you will beg for a sequel
your nose
          nipples and knees
          all parts of the collective people
put the words in a hypodermic
inoculate against Norms
we are about to go exothermic

the words will get you tipsy
like a gypsy
like a ship in a bottle
like Donald you will waddle
like you drank with Captain Morgan
Ray Manzarek on the organ

the words will crawl off the page
black letter ants
will swarm the isle of your rib cage
goose bumping your flesh

as they chew through the mesh
of your red fishnets
freeing the holy mackerel
        the tendrils
of your beautiful legs
so rare they'll be deemed endangered
so hot we'll need a heat exchanger

this poem so silly
your undergarments so frilly
purple and pink water lilies

the words snaking up your spine
moving with rhythm and rhyme
ascending to the height of your bra line
where they will unclasp the latch
Scooby Doo the booby hatch
        and keeping it PG

take a ski
down your belly bee
make you feel
9½ weak in the knees

the words will undress you
        caress you
make you bellow
        wail and cry
make you scream
        holler and sigh

they will leave you nude and anew
your body on the bed askew

like the Leaning Tower of Pisa
leave you with a smile like the Mona Lisa

and with nothing left to say
with nothing left of your body to play
the words will crawl away
back to the crumpled page squished
          in your balled fist
where you sleepily
          and happily lay.

One Poem

It begins like this
with the unbutton of my soul
an unzipping of my skull
dumping everything I have
onto the page
a smearing of colours
every hue
every shade
the pointillism of ideas
images and sounds
clowns
Martha Graham
a Polynesian dance troupe
minestrone soup
the Wizard of Oz
the movie Jaws
the kitchen sink
the hockey rink

it brings in communism
the need to win
revolution
cigar-smoking rebels
Death Stars
automatic cars
the use of force
using The Force

it brings in religion
it brings in tons of fun
crucifixion
the sick son
the holy roller

the Bay City Rollers
ten pin bowler
cross your heart
and hope to strike
while the metaphor is lukewarm
Luke Skywalker
bathwater

I'd get an impeachment
a trail
the fuzz
a fuzzy peach
stream of consciousness
is a bunch of witches
to be put on trial
fuzzy slippers
found guilty

a waste of time
flying out the window
there goes your alarm clock
shouldn't have made her mad
where are those Death Star plans?

super duper
Storm Trooper
storm sewer
everything going to shit
lit
cigarette
never light up around methane
are you insane
this is no game

the court declares a mistrial
somebody is playing a flute
minstrel
tinsel
Christmas
eggnog
a jolly log
Yule log
jolly fat man
dude named Stan
got a fan
come on Han
she is a princess
Cinderella
playing games on the couch
tell me more about your mother

do we now bring in beards
and loaves of bread
hooves of the dead
kicked in the head by a horse
was never the same
autopsy on his brain
funny-looking tumor
heard a rumour
it looked like a boot
Italy
Mussolini
World War III
a place in history
zombie
you'll see

this poem is crazy.

One Poem

This is how it begins
with a bouquet of flowers
your arrival in the world
a celebration
of all the things you will do
experience

        your first steps
        morphing into the foxtrot
        on your wedding day

        more flowers

        a promotion at work

        more flowers

        a trip to the allergist

        less flowers

a series of shots
        poppies
                a farmer in Afghanistan
                        grows them

        some kid will get high
a series of shots

        some kid
                in Gastown
                        will die

this is how it ends
with a bouquet of flowers
your departure from the world

we celebrate all you did
    all you tried to be

yes
this is how it ends
with a bouquet of flowers.

One Poem

As the seasons change
this one and only poem
a still frozen lake.

One Poem

This is how it begins
          with architectural drawings
          schematics
          project software
          timelines

we would begin with a framework
overarching themes
then break it down
poetic project management
art by the pound
multitudinous memes
break it down
in sections
each with their own rhyming structures
focus and context

there would be tankas
and haikus
sonnets
and villanelles

there would be odes
and ghazals
limericks
and epigrams

it would begin here
with this poem
but wouldn't finish for four
                    hundred years
                    Gaudi's cathedral
                    the mission to Jupiter
                    Gran Cavallo

hundreds of notebooks
would travel the globe
with detailed instructions
each different

some
for people to write the saddest
lines of poetry they could think of

for others to write the words
they love
what they know of love
with love

others to write of joy
others of suffering

monks, priests, and rabbis
would write of God

drunks, addicts, and the poor
would write of what it was like
to wake up in the morning
with no hope

deaf people would describe colour
blind people would explain music
they would both express
the ecstasy of red wine

it would take a team of poets
a lifetime to compile it all
to translate it into every language

print it in braille
different groups of musicians
would put different sections of it
to music
an eight-disc set

it would become known as "The Poem"
and it would represent
the world
humanity
freedom
and love

it would be more popular than Dianetics
it would be turned into a Broadway show
and an eccentric billionaire
would turn it into a theme park
in Southern California
        ride The Metaphor
        buy the Bukowski beer
        try your luck at the Word Casino
        win your sweetheart
        a cinquain doll

a hundred years later
The Poem
it would be questioned
panels of academics
would debate its origins
conspiracy theorists would
claim aliens brought it to earth

artists would parody it
a religious movement
would claim it to be heretical
they would send a suicide bomber
to ride The Metaphor
hundreds would die

society would debate
The Poem's value

was it too dangerous?

people would debate it
in bars
waiting for the bus
at the water cooler

then a young girl
age thirteen
would sing a section
of The Poem
on a Taiwanese talent show

it would melt the hearts
of the viewing public
it would be an internet sensation
she would go on to sing
other sections of The Poem
the world tuning in each time
she did

she would win the crown
and an iTune contract to record

The Poem
her version would be the version
which a race of aliens would find
a hundred thousand years
after the human race died

this alien race would study it
and by doing so
it would become part of their flesh
for that's how these creatures
subsisted
their skin the embodiment of ideas

The Poem would be absorbed
into the DNA of the aliens
and it would mutate and spawn
proliferating the galaxy
become part of it

The Poem would
become everything.

One Poem

It begins like this
with the opening
of thick red velvet curtains

in the center of the stage
there is a pulpit
the poet stands behind it
and begins to read

enter stage left
female dancers
dressed in all white body suits
wearing white masks
twirling like Whirling Dervishs

enter stage left
male dancers
dressed in all black body suits
wearing black masks
spinning like tops

they all move behind the poet
looking like a collection
of funnel clouds

the poet takes a dramatic pause
and all the dancers freeze
the poet screams "Engage!"
and the white dancers
leap into the arms of the black

the poet speaks of chess
 of sex
 of yin and yang
 of good and evil
as the dancers dance
 a dance of battle
 of lust
 a tug-of-war of seductions

their bodies smash together
like magnets
pull apart like Silly Putty
their bodies spring and pop
with sensuality
and lust

kink with kink

the poet voice is soothing
like the trickle of a small stream
Ravel's Bolero begins

he speaks about the creation of life
and as he does
the dancers swirl like a gathering storm
until they form a tight circle

out of the centre of the circle
floating up like a magic show
a dancer
dressed in pure red
a flame

the poet speaks of evolution
the changing of the seasons
the metamorphosis of the butterfly

different coloured dancers
erupt from the circle
flowing off the backs
of the other dancers like lava

yellow
            blue
                        green
                                    orange

soon only coloured dancers
remain

the music is building

the poet is now rapping
nonsensical rhymes
            about chaos theory
            Lake Erie
            the lion never gets teary
            the sick of the herd weary
            king of the jungle
            wet boots foot fungal
            met roots bungle
            trip to the Amazon
            bought books on bird spawn
            beaks eating prawns

dancers emerge from the wings
with spots
then some with stripes

as the poet continues to rap
the costumes keep changing
becoming more complex
more colourful
soon they materialize with feathers

    Green-backed Kingfisher
    Orange-banded Flycatcher
    Yellow Weaver

    Blue-faced Rail
    Purple Dollarbird
    Red-breasted Goose

then there is fur
and horns
the music is building
dancers appear on stilts
as elephants
as giraffes

the music is building to crescendo
to a climax

hunters appear in Tilley hats
as the music crashes
they shoot the animals

the dancers limp and roll
in agony
in pain
dancing their dance of death

a coffin is rolled out
and placed behind the poet
he continues to read
as the remaining animals
are killed
as the music finishes

bodies are strewn
all over the stage
surrounding the poet

there is silence
the hunters turn their guns
on the poet

they fire simultaneously
the poet falls into the casket
a hunter closes the door
the rest walk over
lift the box high
and carry it away
          exit stage left

the curtains draw closed

this is how it ends.

One Poem

I would create a monster
a paper maché monster

I would start with a frame
its bones
made from the torn pages
of Bulfinch's Mythology

the muscles would be
paperbacks of Shakespeare
and Goethe

Browning
Wordsworth
Keats and Coleridge
would each get a chamber of the heart

Burroughs would make up the veins
Bukowski the liver
Ginsberg the asshole

the eyes would be crafted from bpNichol
the nose from Irving Layton
the mouth from Lenny Bruce

the brain would be complicated
the frontal lobe Nietzsche
the cerebrum Whitman
the hippocampus Plath
the temporal lobe Brautigan
the amygdala Kerouac
and Edgar Allen Poe the hypothalamus

I would
finish my monster bald
smoothing out his skull
with a clean
blank page

when he was dry
I would take him
to a dark seedy bar
prop him up by the counter
and wait until a drunk
spilled his drink on him

and with this
christening of whiskey
the monster would awaken
like in a fairy tale

he would push the bartender
out of the way
and suck greedily from the beer tap
until he felt soggy

he would squelch his way outside
burp up flowers
and leave oily rainbow footprints
as he trudged deeper towards downtown

he would wander
into a grocery store
and be mistaken
for a bulletin board
he would walk back out

advertising math tutoring
and an apartment for rent

he would wander
into an office building
later coming out covered
in yellow sticky notes

and then
standing on a street corner
he would be shellacked
with a new movie poster
a girl with a nose ring
would tape a notice
about club dates
for a band
named The Electric Tits

he would run into
drunken college students
they would invite him
to their frat house
they would get
my monster drunk
glue pages of pornography
all over his body
and dump him in the park
when he passed out

my monster would awake
be starved for the written word
stumble the length of a writer's block
until he came to a diner

he would order
alphabet soup
and rub his temples
feeling a haiku coming on

he would wander
the street aimlessly for days
sleep on sewer vents
park benches

one morning he would awaken
on the lawn of a high school
kids would be making fun of him
tormenting him
calling him a washed up library

the custodian of the school
would find him duct taped
to the football goalpost
he would free the monster
would hide him
in the basement boiler room
of the school

a nerdy and unpopular kid
would find out the custodian's secret
would visit the monster
in the basement

the monster would like the boy
would rip off his flesh
rip beautiful poems
from his body

and give them to the boy
the boy would show them
to his friends
and they would in turn
show them to friends
and eventually like Head and Shoulders
parents would find out

rumours of a monster
living in the school
preaching subversive poetry
to kids would surface

an angry mob of parent council
would form
would search the school
until the monster was found

then he would be brought
outside
into the basketball yard
they would encircle him
rip poems from his body
read aloud what they deemed to be
the filthy and sick words
that composed his body

there would be a gas can
horrified onlookers
and the tossing of a lit
matchbook

up the monster would go

in flames
his flesh curling black
burnt poems floating up
into the sky

he would try to run
but his legs would turn to ash
and he would fall to the ground
a smoldering pile of soot

the head of the English department
would cry
and everyone would
eventually go home
as the custodian swept up
the mess.

One Poem

It is a snapshot

the coffee maker
doing its spit and hiss
death rattle of the brew
trickling out its last remaining
drops

I pour you a cup
put a little cream in it
like you like

I hand it to you
and then I flip
my remaining crepes
turning them over in the pan
looking like the skins
of burn victims
          perfect

I call our children
to the table
and they come running
to the table
in their pyjamas

the dogs encircle us
waiting for the accidental
windfall

I dole out the syrup
and orange juice
and you pass me the Arts section

from the paper
the music from the iPod plays along
reminding us of something
which puts extra syrup into our smiles

it is everything
the perfect moment
I need nothing more
to say.

One Poem

poem
and only
off of this one
and run and jump
out our parachutes
the top we will pull
and when we reach
before us like a map
our childhood laid out
whole valley floor of
and we can see the
the air begins to thin
and as we climb higher
doo da doo da doo da doo
feathered friends perch and go
upon which the coloured
of the Wild Things protrude
out of which the palm trees
a Tarzan lattice of roots
The Hills Have Eyes
wrinkles of the rocks
up the mountain face
and twist together meandering
and Middle Earth will grow
trees and the woods of Endor
of Lucy's sky and the Avatar
of lady Alice and the flowers
will become like the mushrooms
the more bizarre and exotic the foliage
there could ever be, and the higher we go
every winged beast, hobbit, gnome, elf, and pixie
we will meet every fairy-tale creature that ever was
we will climb this beauty together, and as we ascend
of verse stacked one upon another reaching slowly for the sky
It begins like this, with a foundation, composed of sedimentary lines

One Poem

This poem will leave a stain
on your brain
like Batman on Bane
like Michael on Caine
make you able
tell you a fable
Goldilocks sitting at the table
eating porridge
too hot
            too cold
this poem just right
like a showcase on
the Price is Right
Bob Barker
and the Dark Knight
fighting for animal rights
free a robin
this poem gets your head
bobbin'
gets all the criminals robbin'
this is no joke, sir
here comes the Joker
and the question from the Riddler
make you purr
like Catwoman
so feminine
so much estrogen
modern medicine
it will give you a sex change
make you a new man
part of the master plan
give you a fresh hair do
and a personality like glue

Dave Carnegie has nothing
on you
a hipster
this poem will unstick your zipper
fertilize your library collection
clear up your VD infection
this poem is a shot in your ass
don't Bogart but pass
you know you wanna
smoke marijuana
with Donna
Summer
a nice time to barbeque
smoke in the flue
up goes the house
this poem is a fire ladder
a trampoline catcher
in the Rye
have another drink
pour it down the sink
alcoholism you think
your ring went clink
now the plumber has got crack
working with those pipes
knock knock
who's there?
Johann Sebastian Bach
the plumber found a sock
a little classical on the radio
peer out the window
this poem will mow
your perfect lawn
get you up at dawn

to work on time
to work on time
a watchmaker
making a couch potato
watching the home shopping channel
the neighbour in his sexy flannels
home wrecker with solar panels
enviroman screwing your better half
your lawyer better be getting you half
a little slurry
not to worry
this poem will get you a curry
sing you asleep with Anne Murray
keep you warm
at night
make sure everything is all right
for this is all you'll every need
this poem and a little weed.

One Poem

It begins like this
with a fist
splitting the poet's lower lip
knocking out an incisor

he asks why?

because you're a pathetic
piece of shit
who didn't try

if you could only write
one poem
this is the best you could do?
this is the best you could muster?
so far it's only been lacklustre

put on the tight black gloves
release the John Woo doves
and get ready for the
Stallone punch to the gut
the Chuck Norris roundhouse
and the Patrick Swayze backspin

the poet falls to the ground
spits out a few more teeth
like sunflower seeds

two burly men
like body guards
from a gambling den
pick him up

drag him up the stairs
by the hair
tie him to a chair

here comes the garden shears
and the threat to the digits
by malevolent midgets
to the fingers of the left hand

how many does he need to type?

it's amazing how under duress
suddenly shines his brilliantness
torture him like 1940s Budapest
get him undressed
the whip is carnivorous
leave him with a scar on his chest
in bloody letters it will be expressed
the poet needs to do his best
this is not a request
the poet needs to acquiesce
otherwise he will be laid to rest
we don't want a mess
we don't want regrets
waterboarding gets you wet
so no more threats
write like you had freedom of the press
write until your soul is broken
give us all your raw emotion
on the skin it rubs the lotion
expose everything
with the tide of the ocean
of this one and only poem.

One Poem

It's the warm summer breeze
it's your youth
        the first time a pretty girl
        blew softly into your ear
it's the first album/tape/CD/mp3 you owned
it's the first roller-coaster you went screaming down
it's the first time you found yourself fucking really well
it's the first time you tasted Indian food
it's when you're at a party
        and you say the perfect thing
        because everything is working for you
        like your personality won the lotto
it's when you can see the last six moves to win
        the chess game
it's your wedding day
it's the day your children are born
it's the jump out the window
        into the firefighter net
it's getting more for less
it's getting lucky in parking
it's getting the last one they had
it's getting the full breakfast
it's the feeling when you just wake up
        and the dream lingers in your body
        like you were possessed by a ghost
it's the joy of old friends
        where time isn't a factor
it's jumping into a cottage lake
        and those few seconds of silence
        when the world has been placed on pause
        when all that occurs is a bass blinking at you
it's waffles with strawberries freshly picked from the garden
        and whipped cream not from the can

it's the just missed
        and happy to be alive
it's cuddling on the couch
        with popcorn and a monster movie
it's every favourite moment
        you have ever had
                and ever will have
it's in this
        one and only poem.

One Poem

The poet was depressed
every time he sat down
at the keyboard

the blank page
overwhelmed him
like he was standing
atop a parapet
overlooking the world
everything there before him
all the colours
his childhood
his youth
shopping flyers
religion
fighting with a can opener
cosmogony
death

it was all too much
to try and place into
pieces
place into jars and label them
he tried to write that
write about how overwhelmed
he was
but that too was far too
overwhelming

he went to the bar
sat at the bar
and ordered a beer

a few drinks in
and then a few more
moving towards
a stumble
a woman
built with every floor
a penthouse
excavated
the barstool
next door

she said hi
the poet said jump
she laughed
and said he looked down
he said he was having a hell of a time
with gravity
she laughed again

she asked if he was a writer
he asked how she knew
she said she used to date one
he said how romantic
she laughed again

she said she
could help him
with what he asked
his writer's block
how he asked

she pulled a locket
from her deep cleavage

like she was pulling
a monster from a well

she sprung the latch
and the silver door snapped open
revealing a brown bean

is that ecstasy asked the poet
no
it's a magic bean
and I'll give it to you
if you sleep with me
said the woman

the poet ordered two shots
of Jack
and said he would be happy
to climb her beanstalk

the poet awoke
to painful sunshine
and the bean
on the pillow
where the woman
used to be

he picked it up
and scoffed
magic bean my ass
and out the window it flew
landing in his garden below

that night it rained
and the little bean took root
and it grew and grew and grew
and the next day
when the poet awoke again
he went to his kitchen
and looked out his window
and nearly spilled his coffee

there before him
stood a plant
or was it a tree?
in his garden
like nothing he had every seen
before

it was something out of Dr. Seuss
it was Star Trek vegetation
it was like a sunflower
and palm tree
and an apple tree
and a tulip
communally cross pollinated
into this vine-bush-willow

he immediately remembered
the bean
as he stepped outside to closer
inspect it

hanging off of its branches
were dark purple fruit
which were the size of mangoes
their skin the fuzziness of kiwis

he snapped off a large piece of fruit
brought it into his kitchen
tossed it onto the cutting board
and took a cleaver to it
splitting it into two
weeble wobble halves

the flesh of the fruit
was watermelon red
the pit was a golf ball
and tucked inside
of this hollow seed was a miniature scroll
like a fortune from a cookie

the poet unwound the tiny paper
and to his utter amazement
there were words printed there

he read

it was the most beautiful
collection of words
he had every encountered
and it brought him to tears

he ran out and picked
the rest of the fruit
swaddling the purple pods
in his bunched shirt
like a newborn baby

and as he had hoped
when he split the next
another small parchment

was lodged in the pit
of the fruit

it was another poem
just as elegant
just as moving
just as beautiful
as the first

crimson juice
dripped off the counter
as the perfume of this sweet nectar
soaked the air
while the poet
murdered the rest

with his hands stained elderberry
he typed out the poems
onto his computer
with the fury of a mad scientist
on the edge of a breakthrough

when the poet awoke the next day
the plant-tree had grown another
batch of fruit
and again the poet picked
chopped and transcribed
all the poems he found

after a month of this
he had a manuscript's worth
of material

he entitled it
"Poems Found Inside Magical Fruit"
and sent it to his publisher

within six months
the book came out
to rave reviews

the poet was declared
by many of his peers
to be the greatest living poet
working today

they labelled him a genius

the next year
he took home the Trillium
won the Governor General's
and was anointed the Griffin

everyone kept asking him
what he was working on next

he didn't tell a soul

he had been amassing
poems which he had harvested
from his magic plant

his house persistently stank
of the fruit's sweet sap
a kind of over ripe honeydew
with hints of strawberry
and a slight odor of cheap perfume

hornets wasps bees and flies
relentlessly encircled his refuse
neighbours whispered rumours
of a pot farm

one day the cops showed up
and the poet let them in
and after looking around
they found nothing
didn't even remark
on the bizarre looking tree
in the backyard

but this made the poet very nervous
very nervous indeed

he had enough poems
for twenty more volumes
enough to ensure
his place in the pantheon
of great writers
and he worried someone
might find out about his
enchanted plant
may find out his secret

he went to his garage
found his hacksaw
and went to the back garden
to cut down the magic tree

"I'm sorry," he said
kneeling at its base

placing the teeth of the saw
against the avocado-coloured
bark

the first stroke barely scratched
its bumpy flesh
it was the fourth stroke
in which the saw sliced
into the meat of stock
and from the wound
gushed a thick spray
a gelatinous glue
an alien slime
thick as corn syrup
which stunk of peppermint

it coated the poet's face
and hand
he tried to wipe it away
but the goo quickly hardened
like cement
it sealed the poet's lips together
his left eye in mid-blink
and the fingers of his right hand

the cut in the plant emitted
another spurt of liquid
this time
freezing the poet to the ground
he tried to scream
he squirmed trying to wiggle free
useless

that's when he saw it
the large leaves at the back
near the fence
they moved

and like The Little Shop of Horrors
these leaves moved over
the poet's head
and they parted
revealing teeth
and a grotesque purple tongue

the poet blinked in horror
as the plant
bit him in half
swallowed
and then ate the rest of him

over the next week
the plant grew only one
piece of fruit
a huge purple bulb
the size of a large watermelon

it grew too big for the plant
and eventually it snapped off

its own weight caused it
to split open
when it hit the ground

if anyone had found it
if anyone had cracked open the pit inside
of that final piece of fruit
they would have found
a poem
entitled “One Poem”

but nobody did
and the fruit
and the pit
and the poem
rotted away
forever gone

the tree withered and died
and a malicious computer virus
cleaned out the poet’s hard drive
before anyone could find those fruit poems

somewhere an attractive woman
was walking into a bar
with a silver locket
around her neck.

One Poem

What kind of Dan Millman nonsense is this anyway? Can we really expect excellence in everything we do? Can we expect artists to really do their best every time out of the gate? When we buy a ticket to the fair and there is only one roller coaster, what are we supposed to do for the rest of the day, eat candyfloss? Surely we can't expect people to pay $17.95 for 80 pages of thoughtless babble? Why not be prepared for rhetorical questions? Do artists always put in 100%? Can we assume that? I say we are on the honour system. Then how do we keep score? Do we chalk up the failures and the Manzoni all-too-real copycats to brain damage? Maybe poor artistic training? Heavens to Betsy, could it be laziness after all? Some people have a gift somebody once said. Here is what I say to you with my diamond studded bullhorn, here is what I'm shouting like the carnival barker, "Step right up and GIVE IT YOUR ALL!" This is the once around the park trip, this is the one for all the marbles, this is the whole kit and kaboodle, this is your life, your art. Are you really going to walk away half full of perspective or was it half empty of imagination? Get the correct size of canvas I say. Work it with zeal, work it until you cry because you can't give of yourself anymore. That's when you get up and keep going, that's what separates those who are artists from those who just like the idea of being an artist. And if you already have a trophy on your mantel, remember it's not a life-preserver and you don't lay golden eggs. Your shiny orb is a reminder not to be lax. It's there to remind you of what you are capable of when you push yourself, when your head is not full of ego bubbles and gin. It's about writing every poem as if it were the last thing you were going to say, as if it would be chiselled on your tombstone. This is not a poem. This is all I have to say.

One Poem

The poet had seen the estate sale
walking by on the weekend

on garbage day
he found a box of old photographs
curbside

he took them

the next several weeks
were spent looking
learning them
like tarot cards
shuffling them
with a magician's touch

he made up their names
fabricated their stories
became obsessed with them

he tacked the pictures
all over his bedroom wall
numbered them
like a detective
hunting a serial killer

#37
Aunt Genie
rising her bulbous rump
out of a chair
in polyester pants
with a Jell-O mold cake
in her arms

offering it out-of-frame
while Uncle Paul sat
on the brown couch
in mid-blink
stuffing his pipe

#44 the red-eyed dog named Slippers who was always a rascal
#57 the Christmas turkey and the drunk neighbour Stan
with his rum and coke and comments about immigration

for the most part
the compositions were lousy
nothing properly framed
many were the works of Conner
the child with autism
seen rarely in a few pictures (#85 #92 and #122)
a camera around his neck
like Vivian Myer

this was Conner's family
the Marshals

the poet began a series of poems
about them
their lives
their dreams
their tragedies

Grandpa Lars and the time
he stayed over night with a man of God
molested while Jesus and his mom
watched from the dresser #10

the trickling impact
the lasting effects
the drinking
the beating of his son Andy #12

Andy's secular upbringing
his stint in the army #45 and #67
marrying Liz #70
their kids
        Conner
        Max
        and baby Janet #80

Andy's post traumatic stress
        with a handlebar moustache #98
the stint in rehab with the large lapels #99
the affair with tight slacks #111
the divorce with a new haircut #123
the new girlfriend with a tight handle #156

Conner's lens
caught it all
and the poet
made it all
up

after years of mapping out
the Marshals
writing their stories
their dreams
their failures
their deaths
the poet had a manuscript

he entitled it "The Marshals"

after it was published
it didn't receive much notice

one day
there was a knock
a man stood on the poet's doorstep
he said he was Conner
and that it was his family in those photographs

Conner's real name was Paul
he wasn't severely autistic
but he had Asperger's

the story came out
it went national
it went viral

the poet and Paul
went on talk shows
did radio interviews

the poet was always
so surprised
how much he had gotten
correct about the Marshal family
which really was the Smith family
    the cast on Max's arm #88
    really did come from the mishap
    with the pump at the cottage

one day
Paul didn't show up
when they were to meet
for lunch

calls went unanswered
messages went unreturned
Paul was nowhere to be found

two weeks later
there was a knock
on the poet's door

a woman
stood there
and explained

she was Paul's mother
Paul didn't have Asperger's
he was bipolar
those photographs
were not his family
he lied
made it all up
just like the poet had

Paul was in the hospital
after disrobing on a public bus
after defecating in the aisle

the poet went to see him
in the hospital

anger flew out the window
and they formed a new relationship

once in the hospital
Paul asked the poet
"If you could write only one last poem
          what would you write?"

the poet thought long and hard about it
he sat down and spent
the next twenty minutes writing

after
Paul read it
and a single tear
fell from his right eye

they found him the next day
hanging in the bathroom
from a belt
the poem pinned to his shirt

the poet wrote a non-fiction book
about his relationship
with Paul and their crazy adventures
together

the poet entitled it "One Poem."

One Poem

This is everything
all my thoughts
wrapped up for you

grey matter on a platter
everything I wanted to say
but couldn't
every kiss left behind
the smell of Christmas baking
the sand between your toes
the suck and pull of the tide
            mermaids drinking the water
            between your ankles
            memory washing away

I place it all in the box
all in this poem
the one and only poem

it doesn't cure cancer
it doesn't change the batteries
            in the smoke detector
but it is everything
like watching your children be born

it is all I can give to you

Van Gogh's ear
Rick Allen's arm
Einstein's brain

I gently wrap them
like fish 'n chips
in yesterday's news
and place them in the box
sprinkle them with rose petals
stolen from a Hindu wedding
packed them all with a gold-plated record
foam macaroni
and ideas of God

I wrap the box with cream paper
which creases like good taste
only money can buy
and I tie it
with the reddest of ribbon
and place it
under your tree
where the cerebral inchworm
makes his way along a branch

I walk away
don't look back
smiling

my heart
bursting with love.

One Poem

I was walking
along the beach
when I picked up a stick
and inspiration struck

I carved a poem
into the sand

it was the greatest poem
I'd ever written

arguably the greatest poem of my life

after
I walked on
leaving my poem behind
scrawled there
in the
sand

the next day I walked the same section of beach
and I came to the place
where I'd written my poem

the tide had removed any trace of it
and I thought
perfect.

Acknowledgements

To you, the reader—it just doesn't work without you, so thank you for taking the time to read.

A huge amount of gratitude to Chris Needham who keeps believing in my work. Word.

My readers, Michael Dennis, Ross Buskard, Jeff Hodgson, Nicole Hillmer, and in memory of George Sneyd (1935-2016)—thank you all.

My mother, Judith Gustafsson—couldn't do it without you. Big bear hug.

A very special thank you to Lisa Gegoire for her insight. The next beer is on me.

My wife, Marty, and our kids, Molly and Henry, like it says in the front, this book is for you.